From HEAVEN *Through* NATURE

Holy Spirit Downloads for Divine
Instruction & Encouragement

SESHA JACKSON-WOODARD

Copyright © 2022 Sesha Jackson-Woodard

Scripture quotations marked "KJV" are taken from the Holy Bible, King James Version (Public Domain). All rights reserved. No part of this document may be reproduced or transmitted in any form or by any means, electronic, mechanical, photocopying, recording, or otherwise, without prior written permission of the author.

FROM HEAVEN THROUGH NATURE
Holy Spirit Downloads for Divine Instruction & Encouragement

Sesha Jackson-Woodard
info@droppingseedsinmotion.com

ISBN 978-1-949826-45-6

Printed in the USA.
All rights reserved

Published by: EAGLES GLOBAL BOOKS | Frisco, Texas
In conjunction with the 2022 Eagles Authors Course
Cover & interior designed by DestinedToPublish.com

A devotional that exemplifies God's divine creation for instruction, encouragement and spiritual life application, with personal instances of how Holy Spirit has provided instructions and encouragement. Gain spiritual insight by learning how to pay attention to the fullness of all things God has created and planted on earth.

Sesha Woodard
EITI Authors 2022
info@droppingseedsinmotion.com

Foreword

In this anointed work, Sesha humbles herself and allows the Holy Spirit of God to write through her. With her deep love for God and His blessed creation, she paints a picturesque view that invites the reader to bask in His wonderful presence. The Lord uses Sesha to captivate the reader by showing us the Father in various aspects of nature, with an almost childlike innocence. Her description of God's creation reminds us that each day is a gift from God wrapped in the package of His glorious world. Through the struggle and pain of life shines God's beautiful sun, His voice traveling along the gentle breeze, and the breaking of day as a reminder of His presence! This devotional is indeed an invitation to experience From Heaven, Through Nature.

Pastor Donald R. Pearsall
Healing Touch International Church, Inc.
Raleigh, NC

Dedication

I would first like to dedicate this devotional to my almighty God, the Master Creator! You are truly the DIVINE ARTIST and MASTER SCIENTIST! I also dedicate this book to my family. To my college sweetheart, who is my husband of 16 years: your support and encouragement have been AMAZING. To my fun and awesome kids: you all inspire me and keep me laughing on a daily basis! To my earthly dad, in heaven: you showed me how to enjoy nature just as much as you did. To my mom in heaven: the positive words and seeds, spoken and unspoken, that you planted are sealed in my heart forever. To my sister: I always appreciate your support. I also dedicate this book in memory of a very close high school friend,

Dedication

Munchie. You and I both, as believers in Christ, had a love for nature. Our passions for nature were real, and it was fun loving nature and God's creation with you while you were here on earth.

Acknowledgments

I would like to thank Marilyn Alexander at Destined to Publish and her team for their dedication to this process. Thank you for opening my eyes even more to my own creativity and for helping me to allow my voice to be heard throughout this devotional and to be able to share this experience with others as well.

Thank you to my pastor, Donald Pearsall, and family from Healing Touch International Church for your support and love.

Devotional Outline

Introduction 1

Preface: Prime Your Eyes 9
Day 1 Devotion: The Nest of Holy Spirit 13
Day 2 Devotion: Extended Limbs 17
Day 3 Devotion: Jesus' Footsteps in the Sky. 22
Day 4 Devotion: See the Robustness of Life 27
Day 5 Devotion: The Melody of Morning Birds . . . 31
Day 6 Devotion: What Are You Wrapped or
                        Entangled In? 35
Day 7 Devotion: Shifting Foundations 39
Day 8 Devotion: The Encore of God's Glory. 43
Day 9 Devotion: Cups of Sunshine 47

DEVOTIONAL OUTLINE

Day 10 Devotion: The Divine Artist 51

Day 11 Devotion: The Presence of a Blue Jay. 55

Day 12 Devotion: Run to the Water 59

Day 13 Devotion: Your Walk Is as Unique as
                               You Are 63

Day 14 Devotion: The Stomata of Laughter 67

Day 15 Devotion: The Wind of Holy Spirit. 71

Day 16 Devotion: Arrows of Praise 74

Day 17 Devotion: Rest in Joy 78

Day 18 Devotion: The Sound of Freedom 81

Day 19 Devotion: Blooming in the Midst 85

Day 20 Devotion: Holy Spirit Goes Before Me. . . . 90

Day 21 Devotion: Sent and Set Apart 94

Receive YOUR Devotional Downloads, NOW!. . . . 99

Introduction

A. See the Earth Below

"Okay, here we go! Wheels up! Should I look now? …now? …okay, now." If you have ever flown on an airplane, what you often see after takeoff are passengers gazing through the little oblique window during ascent,

Introduction

descent and even as the captain goes into autopilot. They peer down below at many of the amazing creations made by our almighty God, the ultimate Creator. I too have been in this seat, riding on an airplane, peering out the window in awe of God's creation. This seat is a place of awe, wonder and amazement as I look down on the mighty works of the Master Creator, God!

Whether upon the initial takeoff or when I am soaring through the clouds, I find myself with an eager desire to snap a picture of this amazement, with the intent to solidify the vision and picture of what I have seen through this window. If you are fortunate enough to sit in a window seat on an airplane, it makes it easier to see. But often, there are passengers sitting in the aisle or center seats, and they too are peering toward this oblique window to get a glimpse of what is "down there" or "out there" – looking over my shoulder, shifting back and forth in their seat, hoping to get a glimpse, even if it means only being able to see a portion of life from the window.

Surely, we all know what is below us, right? Earth! And creation! The clouds in all their magnificent forms, land, hills, streams, green grass, ponds and even the tall buildings that God has given man the revelation, insight and wisdom to design and build. Even as I write this, I feel an overwhelming presence and reverence for Father God, our Almighty Creator. I am amazed about the vastness and robustness of *His* tapestry of Earth and even

Introduction

beyond – let's not forget about the entire universe past the clouds. He has so strategically and divinely designed and created it *all*.

So, here we are, on this airplane, above all we have left behind – and the destination we are headed to, for that matter. I think about my mother, who is now in heaven and often said to me, "Write *it* in a book," "You should capture *this* in a book," "*this*" being many of life's ups, downs, successes, triumphs and "aha" moments.

Well, how does what my mother said relate to this devotional about nature and its practical and spiritual life applications, you ask?

B. Experience Nature

I always had a love for nature, and I collected beautiful rocks as a child. While exploring outside, I felt like I wanted to take a little piece of nature with me. I would

Introduction

keep the rocks in my pocket, and my daddy would call me "rock woman." Now that I'm an adult, my currently 11-year-old daughter also sees the beauty in God's creation – and yes, she collects rocks too!

As my relationship continued to grow with Father God and as I continued to receive what Holy Spirit spoke to my heart, I started to see and experience nature in a different way. I thought I was merely appreciating the beauty of all He created, but after a while, I realized Holy Spirit was speaking to my heart in a *different* way. It was like a song. There are some melodies and tunes that draw us in more than others. For me, the landscape of nature is a pictorial melody that draws me in with its own song. In fact, one day just recently, I heard Holy Spirit speak to me and simply but profoundly say: *"I speak to you through nature because you PAY ATTENTION to it."*

What if this was a part of God's plan? Those Selah moments are what my mom was referring to. What if God wants us to do the same? To capture the moments, allow Him to speak to each one of us and keep a rolodex, feed or photo album of memories that speak to our lives and situations so we can use them as learning experiences in that moment and for the rest of our lives. To receive downloads, spiritual truths found in nature that Holy Spirit can use to share practical life application teachings, encouragement, direction and more.

Introduction

As I got older, I learned more about God and how He sent His Son, Jesus, to die on the cross for our sins so that we may live eternally. I learned that Jesus left Holy Spirit here with us to comfort us. I then started to develop more of a relationship with Christ and purposed to be even more connected to Holy Spirit, while at the same time learning and applying His Word to my life.

In this devotional, I share several of my very own experiences with nature and give you the full essence of each one. I walk you through the beautiful ways in which Holy Spirit uses various things in nature to provide instruction, guidance and even encouragement. I pray that each devotion will inspire you to pay attention to nature and look for Holy Spirit to speak to your heart. As you tap into your own melody in nature and listen to Holy Spirit, there is also space at the end of each devotion for you to write or draw what you see from nature and what Holy Spirit shares with you during these special moments. Be open to what God has for you!

I never really thought the situations I experienced were super substantial, but nonetheless, my mom wanted and encouraged me to "capture" these moments of life. At that age, I would just smile when she would mention this and think to myself, "A book? Naw, I have no interest in doing this, Mommy!" But the dynamics of flying on a plane are such that the higher you go in the sky, the

Introduction

more you see. Expand and open your mind as you read through each devotion. Receive and allow the pictures, Holy Spirit downloads and prayers from heaven to flow. Ask Holy Spirit for guidance and instruction. Ask Holy Spirit, "What are you saying to me as I observe these magnificent works of your hands?"

God wants to use His magnificent creation to speak His spiritual truths to you. Allow Holy Spirit to be your guide through this journey of life. If you stop for a moment, put yourself on pause, and look around like we did when we were on that plane, we will see and hear from God, as He uses all things, people and situations to speak to us, including nature. You must be intentional. Give Him your undivided attention. Open your eyes (physical and spiritual)! Look around! See God and His divine instruction everywhere in nature!

Let's go back to the visual of being on a plane. Imagine your life like an airplane, and the wind of Holy Spirit is sending you forth. You don't just get on a plane without knowing where you are going. Do you? Once we accept Jesus Christ as our Lord and Savior, we know (if not immediately, hopefully soon) that God desires to use us to be sent out to do His specific will. Everyone's purpose is different. I encourage you to anticipate beauty in the instruction God will give you by learning how God

Introduction

strategically designed *all* things in nature to operate and flow, whether they are plants, animals, etc.

When the plane reaches its altitude, this is where you quickly take out your cell phone and snap a pic of the beautiful view. Why? It's the same earth that you just left a few minutes before, right? Perhaps it's the different view that intrigues you, or the fact that when the plane ascends above the clouds, it allows you to get a *better* picture of God's Bigger Picture. I am reminded of the following scripture: *"The earth is the Lord's, and the fullness thereof; the world, and they that dwell therein. For he hath founded it upon the seas, and established it upon the floods…"* (Psalm 24:1-2). Seeing God's perspective on a situation is worth more than money or gold, just like what Solomon in the Bible asked for: wisdom (Proverbs 16:16). We obtain clear direction from Holy Spirit, and God can use anything and everything He chooses to speak to His people – yes, even nature, which is the purpose of these 21 devotions.

PREFACE

Prime Your Eyes

My desire for you is to start noticing various things in nature, if you haven't done so already. Allow me to paint a picture: You are standing on the bank near a stream that is moving briskly in one direction. You are now compelled to walk along this bank, and your eyes are drawn to the water – it's like the water is leading you and beckoning you. As you walk along with this stream, with the wind gently blowing and cradling your face, you look off into the distance. The large palm-like leaves on a nearby tree blow in many opposing directions compared to the single direction of the flowing stream you have been following.... And then Holy Spirit speaks to you. You know it is coming straight from God because you immediately sense His presence. And then, here it comes.... Ready? The HOLY SPIRIT DOWNLOAD straight to your HEART.

As you listen to the sound of the water flowing over the rocks of the stream, and embrace the wind gently tickling your cheek as a mother cupping the side of her sleeping baby's face, God speaks to your heart: "Follow the Spirit with which I am leading you. Give ear to my words and direction. Though you see others swaying or moving in different directions, follow my lead as I quicken your spirit to MOVE."

Though your journey may be rocky, like the tiny rocks you see being pushed about in the stream, God is speaking to you now, even in this pictorial moment. Holy Spirit says: *"Just as the water in the midst of the stream flows before you, I will go before you and will be with you and never leave you, nor forsake you* [Deuteronomy 31:8]. *There is purpose for you along the way, and as you complete your Holy Spirit-led purpose on earth, stay connected and remain faithful, because the wind of my Spirit will help you reach and complete ALL I have for YOU!"*

But wait! Did you know that the very nature of how streams flow is that they give way and empty and lead into lakes and oceans? So, just when you think you have finished an assignment, God has more abundance for you (Ephesians 3:20)! I know! What an amazing way to think about it! So, keep walking close to Him, taking in those amazing moments He desires to share in nature with you. You may not live near a stream or even walk close to one in your life, but I used this as an example to show you how Holy Spirit can easily and freely use your own personal experiences with nature to speak to you, download into you and encourage you on your journey.

Now, imagine that you are so in tune that Holy Spirit speaks to you as often as you bask and soak in nature. I'm not just talking about your vacation time, but on a daily basis – just by going about your everyday activities. It doesn't matter what region of the world, hemisphere, continent, state, city, county or street you live in – Holy Spirit desires to engage your senses of sight, touch, hearing and even smell to speak directly to *you*! Yes you! I encourage you to pay attention when you look at and learn about nature, even if it is on a TV program like *Planet Earth* or *National Geographic*. I often like to watch programs on TV that share and discuss various animals, plants and the earth in general. Open your mind and your will today to really experience it all.

DAY 1 DEVOTION

THE NEST OF HOLY SPIRIT

Look at that! It is nestled so firmly. It looks like it's going to fall as it rests on the branches that appear feeble and frail on the barren tree. Looking across the field and through the cold sky of this winter day, I am reminded of how often I actually see nests under these conditions. Look at the next tree and the next tree and the next! There is more, there is so much more that I see! Bird's nests! God strategically leads these birds to specific twigs, stones, branches and leaves to establish their nests.

While we as humans may not be able to understand how in the world the "nuts and bolts" of a perfectly tapestried nest are uniquely and divinely perched, perfectly situated – staying up high, high, high, in these trees on branches without leaves – the bird still trusts the nest it has built. Why? I believe it is the innate and instinctive instruction of God that guides these birds to the "right" materials to use and shows them where to build their home, the nest. Holy Spirit reminds me that as followers of Jesus Christ, we are to listen to God, be doers of the word (James 1:22-25) and allow Him to be our foundation.

Who says you can't build, grow, flourish and be prosperous in a cold, barren situation? Our foundation must be on God's word through Jesus Christ. I hear the birds even louder now as I write, and I feel in my spirit that they are touching and agreeing with me because they know who *their* Creator is as well. It is written that everything that has breath must praise the Lord (Psalm 150:6). The next time you see a bird's nest, think about how God promises to take care of you and give you direction even in the midst of the barrenness that seems to surround you.

Sometimes you may think your foundation will just fall through to the ground, but ask yourself, when was the last time you saw a bird's nest fall from a tree? Every twig, every leaf, every branch and every rock – everything birds use to build their nesting foundation – is symbolic of the divine instruction, guidance and strategy Holy Spirit gives us to build our foundation of strength through living by God's word. Continue to believe and build, and watch your foundation stay firm and solid. Be the dwelling place for Holy Spirit to rest in your nest.

> **Scripture: Matthew 7:24-25** *"Therefore whosoever heareth these sayings of mine, and doeth them, I will liken him unto a wise man, which built his house upon a rock: And the rain descended, and the floods came, and the winds blew, and beat upon that house; and it fell not: for it was founded upon a rock."*
>
> **Prayer:** Lord, I thank you today, and I declare that you are my rock, my foundation and my strength, no matter what may be happening in my home or in my life. Holy Spirit, I pray I will not just hear your word, but take action and *do* the word. I will listen even more attentively for your divine instruction, and I purpose to build the Kingdom of God. When I feel weak, I will remember to trust in your promises

and in every word you speak. Though various situations in my life may look like they are fragile and could crumble and fall at any moment, I will rest my nest in you. In Jesus' Name.

DAY 2 DEVOTION

Extended Limbs

What is that I see to the right? They look like extended hands. You know, like when you're in a Holy Spirit-filled worship service and the person next to you extends out their hands and arms to give God an extension of praise, showing their complete adoration and surrender to Father God. But no, these are not human hands I see extended; they are in fact the limbs of trees, though they resemble the very essence of the hands of a human. Is this just my imagination? In that very moment, I "saw" praise, but not only did I see praise, I heard and felt Holy Spirit say, *"Look, even the trees are reaching to the heavens to praise me"* – "me" being our Almighty Father, God.

Go to that place for a moment: when nothing matters in that very moment but the pull and tug at your heart and spirit to worship the Lord. When you feel God's anointing come over you, the heat of His burning presence and joy that bubbles in the depths of your belly, you feel it cannot be contained. Your arms then extend out and up to glorify the Almighty! I have experienced this sacred place of worship many times in my life as my relationship with God and Jesus Christ has continued to grow over time.

As you get closer to God, He will pour out His Spirit on you even more. Make sure your heart is humble and you ask Him daily for forgiveness of your sins. This keeps your vessel yielded and open to receive. You will feel even more moments throughout your day to offer an extreme arm's-length extension of praise from your heart to Father God in worship. The word of God even says that if we don't cry out, the rocks will (Luke 19:40).

Extended Limbs

Out of all the trees that could capture my attention, Holy Spirit led my focus to this one specific tree, with its extended limbs. What I didn't mention before is that I was actually riding in the car on a highway in North Carolina. Do you know how many trees I see riding these NC highways? Yes, a lot! But in that moment, when I could have blinked and not even noticed this one particular tree, Holy Spirit steered my focus to *this* tree that was vividly displaying how we as believers are to have a strong, powerful, eye-catching stance of praise that can be illustrated in how we simply extend our arms in adoration to God. It's just like I mentioned previously, when your eyes scan across people in the congregation and you see one person who is in total abandonment in worship, just like the tree with its extended limbs, because it doesn't matter what others around them are thinking – their mind, spirit, heart and even their physical body are directed toward Christ and unashamedly giving Him the glory He deserves.

The next time you travel along a highway, road or street, or even if you're out for a walk, look for the extending tree limbs and branches and allow Holy Spirit to extend and communicate with you what He desires. Remember, if you do not offer praise to the Lord, the rocks will cry out. Open your eyes to see the pictorial moments of praise that Holy Spirit shows you through nature – even the trees you may pass daily. Join in with the trees as the praise is being extended to God!

Scripture: 1 Chronicles 16:33 *"Then shall the trees of the wood sing out at the presence of the Lord, because he cometh to judge the earth."*

Prayer: God, I thank you for another day to allow me to extend and offer up praise from my spirit, heart and physical body. May every part of me fully give you glory and honor. Just as the trees you have planted on earth display your glory, I will extend even more praise to you. Allow me to see and experience how great the release of your praise can be and the manifestation of your presence as I release my praise to you today. I pray you are pleased with my sacrifice of praise and overtake me with your presence. In Jesus' Name.

Extended Limbs

DAY 3 DEVOTION

Jesus' Footsteps in the Sky

I was awed at what I saw in the sky that night. Traveling back from my daughter's basketball game, I looked through the front windshield of the car and there it was, the many horizontal hues of pink. They looked like so many different pink colors layered over top of each other like cotton candy, or like a painter who has painted the many shades of a sunset. I looked to the left of this breathtaking sunset and saw painted in the sky what appeared to be footprints. I thought, "The footprints of Jesus!" and in that moment, I imagined Him walking through the sky.

Five minutes after I witnessed this amazing heavenly picture, my uncle called and gave me the news: "Grandma passed today," he said, and the cluster of silence that rested in that moment was just as permeating as those pink clouds I saw a few minutes earlier. I knew this news was coming as soon as I looked at my caller ID. Holy Spirit is a comforter, and Holy Spirit saw fit to show me all those different hues of pink and the "footsteps of God" because He wanted me to be comforted right before I heard this news.

In that moment, Holy Spirit gave me a vision of Jesus coming down from His heavenly throne to meet and escort my grandmother to her heavenly mansion – thus leaving the sky painted with footsteps as a visual comfort for me as he ushered her into heaven. The pink colors I described are so significant in this instance because my grandmother absolutely *loved* the color pink. Every birthday cake I bought her was pink and white – she loved cake too! She was 93 years old when she passed, and pink had been her favorite color for as long as I can remember. In fact, for her homegoing service, she was adorned with a pink dress and pink lipstick, with pink and white flowers all around. I am thankful, and I appreciate the comfort God gave me during that time. He desires to show us that He cares through comforting us. I know at times we may not feel the comfort, but I encourage you to pay close attention to the things around you that may seem little and minute. He can speak volumes to you with the simplest things in nature – simply pay close attention.

Being in tune to nature at all times, no matter what part of the day, from sun up to sun down, will open your senses to Holy Spirit downloads of revelation, insight, knowledge, encouragement and instruction. In this case, for me, it was the peace and comfort that Holy Spirit knew I needed in that moment. Oh yes, and colors are significant, so be in tune to that aspect as well! Look how all the hues of pink spoke to my heart because they related to my grandmother. When was the last time you noticed the colors in the sky? Look for those Holy Spirit-speaking colors today. Use this space after the devotion to write/draw what you see, experience and feel. – Capture these sweet and intimate Holy Spirit moments!

Scripture: 2 Corinthians 1:3-4 *"Blessed be God, even the Father of our Lord Jesus Christ, the Father of mercies, and the God of all comfort; Who comforteth us in all our tribulation, that we may be able to comfort them which are in any trouble, by the comfort wherewith we ourselves are comforted of God."*

Prayer: Father, thank you for the creative ways you speak to me and comfort me as well. Help me to pay even more attention to the details of life that are all around me – from the colors you paint in the sky to the moments in life when you touch my spirit to provide comfort in times of need. May my spirit always be in tune and open to hear your heart and receive whatever YOU know I need in that very moment. In Jesus' Name.

DAY 4 DEVOTION

SEE THE ROBUSTNESS OF LIFE

Like Day 2, this next Holy Spirit download is also related to trees, but it's a bit different. It's amazing how Holy Spirit can use a similar example in nature – in this case, trees – to speak different spiritual truths. When you look at nature, I encourage you to be open minded, because Holy Spirit may speak something totally different to you through a similar observation in nature – so keep your eyes and your heart open!

While riding in the car on the highway (so thankful my husband likes to drive while I take in the scenery), I looked to the right and saw barren trees. It is winter as I write this particular devotion, so I do expect to see trees without leaves, of course, but there is one that clearly stands out – it's likely an evergreen tree because the branches stand out with their super green color. Evergreen trees stay green all year long due to their ability to conserve more water despite the cold months of the winter, in contrast to other trees that lose their leaves in colder months.

Why would God plant an evergreen tree right in the midst of trees that would eventually lose their leaves? Perhaps so that someone like myself would recognize the spiritual instruction in this moment and share it with you for revelation and encouragement. Holy Spirit revealed that this evergreen tree represented the life we should exhibit in the midst of darkness, trials, struggles and tribulation – even if we are among people with negative attitudes at school, work, etc. Holy Spirit continued to download to my spirit that the leaves on the branches, extending from your heart, stand out and dance among the barrenness, causing the darkness and negativity to be drowned out by the surrounding life.

People can usually see and feel if you are carrying the light of Christ. Why? Because if you are standing firm in Christ and are completely yielded to Him, you inevitability carry life. In fact, life and light should be shining from you so brightly that people squint their eyes when they are in your presence. But really, people should feel the presence of God such that there is a draw which Holy Spirit can use as an opportunity to minister to whomever is in your presence.

There may be circumstances and situations where the only light of Christ people pass by will be *you*. When they see you, they see the green abundance and the life-giving power of Christ. They see the robustness God planted in you. Stand out today, and yes, you may be the only one in the midst of barren branches, but God strategically placed you there for a purpose! Keep flourishing!

> **Scripture: 2 Corinthians 4:6** *"For God, who commanded the light to shine out of darkness, hath shined in our hearts, to give the light of the knowledge of the glory of God in the face of Jesus Christ."*
>
> **Prayer:** Father, I thank you for your life-giving presence in my life. Thank you for sending your son, Jesus Christ, to be my Savior. Help me continue to yield to your will. As I encounter situations in my life where there may be

See The Robustness Of Life

barrenness all around, I pray your light will shine forth through me for others to see so that they may be drawn to you. Open the door of opportunity for me to share your love and even an encouraging word to those you place in my presence today. In Jesus' Name.

DAY 5 DEVOTION

The Melody of Morning Birds

I woke on a Friday morning to the lullabies and praises of the birds singing right outside my bedroom window. The melody and brilliant orchestra of these birds lifted

The Melody Of Morning Birds

my spirits as I lifted my eyelids and thanked God for another new morning. I wondered what these birds think about in the morning. I wondered if their hearts cry out in thanks to the Father as well. The Word says, *"Let every thing that hath breath praise the Lord"* (Psalm 150:6), and by the sound of these birds, it was clear that the breath of God dwelled in them.

I was tuned in now to the long note that one bird released in the atmosphere – almost as if to warn me not to hit the snooze button again and inform me that it was time to get up and join in the melody of the morning. It is true that God's joy comes in the morning. There is a freshness in the air in the morning, a covering, like a blank slate, a new start, and I was hearing these birds singing as if there was nothing else going on at that moment in time but their oneness with God, our Father, the Creator. Nothing mattered at that time but the sound that was being sent into the atmosphere at that very moment. Such peace.

What sound are you sending through the air waves in your atmosphere when you wake in the morning? Are you complaining about another issue, or have you made up your mind to put it in God's hands and leave it there? Do you allow the songs of the morning to pull and draw you into His presence? Release the joy from your heart. Even if you don't feel joyous, sing anyway. Hum anyway.

Bless the Lord, oh your soul, worship His Holy name (Psalm 103)! You will find that your own personal melody of permeating praise will stay with you throughout your morning and the rest of the day. Keep singing! Join in with the birds!

> **Scripture: Psalm 103:1-4** *"Bless the Lord, O my soul: and all that is within me, bless his holy name. Bless the Lord, O my soul, and forget not all his benefits: Who forgiveth all thine iniquities; who healeth all thy diseases; Who redeemeth thy life from destruction; who crowneth thee with lovingkindness and tender mercies."*
>
> **Prayer:** Father, I wholeheartedly thank you and bless you for your grace and mercy. Those times when I feel like complaining, moaning and groaning, I pray you would help me to instead bless you and think more about the benefits of developing an intimate relationship with you. Help me to fix my heart on the melodies of your goodness. In Jesus' Name.

The Melody Of Morning Birds

DAY 6 DEVOTION

WHAT ARE YOU WRAPPED OR ENTANGLED IN?

You can either be entangled in the things of God and His protection or in the things of the enemy. When you see trees with branches wrapped around them, do you ever wonder where and how these branches actually grow around a tree like this? Most often, I have seen these branches start at the bottom of the tree, near the roots. So, imagine this: if the enemy wanted to get to the

What Are You Wrapped Or Entangled In?

foundations of your salvation – your unadulterated belief, hope and passion for Jesus Christ – where would he start? If you've ever experienced times in your life when you questioned your faith and wondered if the Lord really heard your prayers, well, don't be ashamed, this has happened to many seasoned believers. The important thing is that you recognize this and take these thoughts captive (2 Corinthians 10:5); purge them with the unwavering doctrine of Jesus Christ and stand firm as a tree planted by the rivers of waters (Psalm 1:3).

So, I ask: What entangles you? What appears to have a hold on you? What are you wrapped in? I say it again: You are a tree planted by the rivers of waters. The beautiful thing about trees is that they are exposed to and experience all the various elements of nature, including the storming gusts of wind, blazing tropical sun rays and ice-cold raindrops. When we look at trees and how they usually just seem to simply stand, no matter what the circumstance, we recognize that they are strategically built for the elements of nature. God was fully aware of the elements the trees would experience, so He has given them a covering of protection to withstand those elements.

You may be asking how this translates to your life. The enemy gets frightened when he sees you – God's firmly planted tree, covered and entangled in the branches of His protection. He may want to get to you but does not know where to start, just like figuring out where to start to untangle someone's hair.

So, how much more protection would God give you? Here is what Holy Spirit is speaking about this massive tree wrapped with branches: *"The moment you accepted me (Jesus Christ) as your Lord and Savior, I sent my wrapping of protection over you and around you. I encapsulate you with my love. I am the one that gives you strength. I am the one that protects you from the adversary. The entanglement of protection is indicative of how much I love you and am purposed to support you now and forever. My branches of love for you are so powerful and intricate that you cannot see where they start and end – but be at peace with this, as I am the God of peace. I will continue to uphold you with my right hand. You will not stumble, even if you appear to. You are rooted in me, and when the enemy comes in like a flood, I promise to lift up a standard on your behalf* [Isaiah 59:19]."

Scripture: Psalm 3:1-3 *"Lord, how are they increased that trouble me! many are they that rise up against me. Many there be which say of my soul, There is no help for him in God. Selah. But thou, O Lord, art a shield for me; my glory, and the lifter up of mine head."*

Prayer: Father, thank you for the entanglement of your protection, for helping me stand firm in you and on your word. Continue to show

What Are You Wrapped Or Entangled In?

me love throughout this day and beyond. You are helping me to understand the vastness of the great love and protection you have for me. Thank you for your love and everlasting protection. In Jesus' Name.

DAY 7 DEVOTION

SHIFTING FOUNDATIONS

While my husband and I were visiting a potential house to purchase, I got out of the car and noticed beautiful roots nestled firmly in the ground on the somewhat grassy area next to the house we were visiting.

I followed the path to see where the source of these roots were coming from. They led straight back to a beautiful tree that was firmly planted next to the sidewalk. You could tell the tree had been planted many years ago. The house was built in 1935. As I stood next to this tree, I wondered and thought to myself, "How far do these roots reach? How deep into the earth do these roots really go?" In that moment, I thought, "If I could only be a hedgehog and dig into the earth to put my wondering to rest."

As my husband and I walked through the house, we noticed that the floors in many areas of the house were tilted. We speculated that the massive roots of the tree on the sidewalk perhaps made its way underneath the house, pushing the foundation and in essence shifting the house. From outside the house, we could not see the depth of the impact of the roots and how they had shifted the house until we actually walked through.

In that moment, Holy Spirit downloaded a spiritual truth to me. Sometimes the roots of our past affect our future and we don't see it, or we don't understand the impact of leaving the roots of an issue unaddressed and unattended. Years go by and the negativity of this shift is still there, interrupting and protruding through your relationships, your purpose… your life. Sometimes, it takes someone else just simply walking through your "house" (the house of your heart) to notice a shift. The beautiful thing is that it can be fixed and mended! Yes, I am referring to the house and to your heart! My husband and I realized that the shifting floors could be repaired by having a professional lift up the house.

Holy Spirit says: *"You do not need to lead an unbalanced life. Even though deeply rooted situations that occurred in your life may have caused a shift in where you stand today, be lifted by 'The Professional': Jesus Christ, who was sent into the earth so His people can live abundantly. I can get to the root of where you are off balance and supernaturally lift the trauma, anxiety, fear and hurt from your past. You may see brokenness now, but wait until I work my nurturing love – in your house, and on your heart. Be ready and open to receive from me. Once the house of your heart is lifted, the sun will shine evenly in and through each and every chamber of your heart and in every area of your life. You will walk in wholeness and balance!"*

>**Scripture: Matthew 11:28-30** *"Come unto me, all ye that labour and are heavy laden, and I will give you rest. Take my yoke upon you, and learn of me; for I am meek and lowly in heart: and ye shall find rest unto your souls. For my yoke is easy, and my burden is light."*

Prayer: Father, I know you desire for me to be whole in every area of my life. The truth is, I need you to come into my life, into my heart. In fact, I need you to help heal me from those issues that occurred in the past that have taken root in my life – things I may not even be 100% aware of myself. You are the lifter of my head. I ask for you to help me to receive the wholeness and balance in my life that you promise in your Word. In Jesus' Name.

DAY 8 DEVOTION

THE ENCORE OF GOD'S GLORY

"Spring is almost here!" I think as I sit in this coffee shop and write. The walls are orange, which brings a feeling of "life" to the atmosphere. I sit in my usual seat, close to the door, so I can catch the breath of fresh air that sweeps in each time someone swings open the door to enter or leave. Once I order my coffee (super-hot salted Hawaiian caramel coffee with *lots* of whip cream – my favorite), I walk back to my cozy working nook, look outside the window and notice that the outside view is different. The trees next to the parking lot are blooming with beautiful white flower buds! It's the month of March when I am writing this, and among the busyness of life, between basketball games, cheer and the many other exciting activities my children are involved in, I see this view and, here in this very moment, ultimately realize the spring season is just around the corner.

What do you think about when you see spring flowers blooming? You may think about warmer weather, planting flowers or even a special vacation you'd like to take. For me, the onset of spring is like God pulling back the curtain for an encore – presenting the cast just one more time after a magnificent theater production.

Holy Spirit speaks to us through the changes in seasons. As wives, husbands, parents, etc., sometimes we can get caught up in our to-do lists, errands, meals to prepare and just the everyday stuff that life can bring. I encourage you to anticipate "The Great Encore." It's the time when you can clearly notice that the seasons are in the process of changing. Just when things around you start to look the same, *swoosh!* The curtain of God's creation suddenly reveals the extraordinary splendor. Let it be a reminder for you to pause from the busyness of life to enjoy the encore of God's glory.

Scripture: Psalm 145:5-6 *"I will speak of the glorious honour of thy majesty, and of thy wondrous works. And men shall speak of the might of thy terrible acts: and I will declare thy greatness."*

Prayer: Father, I thank you for the beauty and splendor you have planted in the earth. Help me to find moments to pause for an encore, to take in the view around me and the different fragrances of the season. I desire to revere you and acknowledge the majestic glory you have created. When life gets busy, allow me to pause for an encore. In Jesus' Name.

The Encore Of God's Glory

DAY 9 DEVOTION

Cups of Sunshine

Yes, I am in the coffee shop again. Have you ever been in a room, maybe even asleep, when someone comes in and abruptly turns on the light, then turns it off, then turns it back on again? How would you respond? Depending on the situation, you may respond in a curious or confused way – wondering why anyone would do such a thing, especially if you were comfortable and nestled in a deep, cozy sleep. Perhaps in this situation, the person manipulating the light may be trying to get your attention.

Well, this is what I experienced in the coffee shop today as I was deeply focused on my work. No one turned the actual lights off, then on and then off again as I previously described – in this case, the beams of light actually came from the sunshine. In an instant, the illuminating rays from the sun saturated the coffee shop as if someone had just turned the knob to the highest illumination setting. And then the sunlight dimmed again, and as the wind blew outside, this illuminating light from the sun disseminated once more. God turned up the dimmer to its highest setting, and the sun rays beamed through to where I was sitting.

In that illuminating moment, Holy Spirit downloaded straight to my heart: *"I am getting your attention, waking you up to my glory, shining bright on creation and waving the sun rays of glory for all humanity to see."* Holy Spirit allowed these rays to beam in a matter of seconds in my presence, and in such a sequential, methodical flow that I felt Holy Spirit was speaking directly to me. In that moment, I wondered if anyone else around me even noticed. I stopped, basked in those moments of illuminating rays that pushed through the sky and offered up a praise to God.

Holy Spirit doesn't just want to speak to *me*. I believe God desires to commune with you in this way as well. God is encouraging you to stop, look up, see, feel and experience the heavenly downloads from the heart of Father God as you go about your day.

Scripture: Matthew 5:16 *"Let your light so shine before men, that they may see your good works, and glorify your Father which is in heaven."*

Prayer: Father, I realize you desire to speak and commune with me in a different way than what I am used to. I may not fully understand the steps to take or how this will even occur, but I submit to hear from you in a different way – through my observations of all you have created. I commit to being in tune with nature. May you direct me to what you desire for me to observe. I pray now for clarity in what you show me, and I thank you in advance for speaking to my heart in a mighty way. In Jesus' Name.

Cups Of Sunshine

DAY 10 DEVOTION

THE DIVINE ARTIST

My dog Sparkle wears a jacket. Not a real jacket, but she is gray and white and the top part of her coat luxuriously drapes to midway down her front and back paws. She literally looks like she is wearing a cape or a robe. But the Master Artist did not stop there – the tip of her tail looks like it was dipped in white chocolate. I mean, it literally looks like her fur was intentionally crafted to look like this – as if someone meticulously crafted the design. If the Master Creator took His time and applied intricate details to create the loving dogs we graciously make our family members – and cats too (if that is your preference) – how much more thought, care and attention does our God put into creating us, His people, a chosen generation?

He made you a little lower than the angels (Psalm 8:4-5). This means you have rank and position in God's Kingdom. No one can pull or remove you from this Kingdom position. You are fearfully and wonderfully made.

Sparkle is still here with her beautiful coat, but now we have a new puppy, Stella. Stella is gray and brown with the cutest little light brown eyebrows. They actually look like little dots of brown sugar. My nine-year-old son shared with me that when he looks at Stella's eyebrows, they remind him of Skittles candy, which is his favorite candy, by the way. How cute!

When I see the intricacies of the animals like the black and white zebra with its electrifying stripes, or the dynamic, rich color of a blue jay or red robin, I am reminded by Holy Spirit that every – and I mean *every* –

single detail of God's creation is blueprinted by His Master Design. The next time you look at an animal, I encourage you to look closely at the color, design and pattern that God has uniquely bestowed on each, and remember that He also made you unique and intentionally different with your own gifts, talents and beauty – *all* for His Glory.

> **Scripture: Psalm 139:14** *"I will praise thee; for I am fearfully and wonderfully made: marvellous are thy works; and that my soul knoweth right well."*

> **Prayer:** Father, you are miraculous in all your ways and in all you created. How wonderful and miraculous it is to see your handiwork. You are the Master Artist! Help me continue to see the art of your heart in all you created. In Jesus' Name.

The Divine Artist

DAY 11 DEVOTION

The Presence of a Blue Jay

As I sit here and work from home, I look outside to a beautiful day, and once again, I see what I believe to be the same blue jay that has been hanging out in my back yard for the past couple weeks. But now this blue jay is propped up on one of the pillars of the fence in my back yard. Its color is so vibrantly blue that I cannot help but peer in awe at this beautiful bird. Colors have biblical significance, and blue represents the Heavenlies and Holy Spirit, so I wondered at that moment what Holy Spirit wanted to download to my heart.

And then, just as gracefully as this blue jay glided by and perched on top of the fence, Holy Spirit spoke in a distinctly loud voice: *"Every time you look up, I am there as the Lord, your God, present, resting and perched in the midst of your situation. When you go about your day, I am in the midst of you, flying through the air and perching in your presence to remind you of the holy and heavenly manifestation of my glory in your life."* This blue jay only stayed perched on my fence for a few seconds, but in those few seconds, Holy Spirit spoke comfort and revelation that some preachers would spend upwards of an hour or so delivering.

I do enjoy a good sermon, but God wants to continue to speak to you beyond the Sunday-morning preaching from the pulpit. He wants you to be able to recognize the Holy Spirit download moments where He can show you the beauty of His creation and in the same moment give you encouragement, direction, clarity or peace, or simply compel you to stand in awe and amazement of His remarkable works! So, pay very close attention to the nature that surrounds you on a daily basis. Sometimes Holy Spirit only needs a few seconds to give you that on-time Holy Spirit download you need to make it to the next day, hour or even moment.

Scripture: Psalm 139:7-10 *"Whither shall I go from thy spirit? or whither shall I flee from thy presence? If I ascend up into heaven, thou art there: if I make my bed in hell, behold, thou art there. If I take the wings of the morning, and dwell in the uttermost parts of the sea; Even there shall thy hand lead me, and thy right hand shall hold me."*

Prayer: Father, I thank you for being everywhere at all times, just like all you have created in the earth. It does not just disappear. The trees you planted, the very air you release into the atmosphere, the light and sun you shine on me daily from the sky – it is all here, and you have promised you will never leave me or forsake me. As I take in the constant presence of nature, may I also always be reminded of the omnipresence of your Spirit. You are with me at all times. Thank you! In Jesus' Name.

The Presence Of A Blue Jay

DAY 12 DEVOTION

Run to the Water

I don't really watch a lot of television, but if you were to find me watching TV, you would see the show *Our Planet* or something from National Geographic on the screen. When I watch these programs and hear the narrator explain the magnificent phenomena of nature in all its synergistic flow, I feel like I am immersed in the midst of the Glory of God's creation.

One day, I was watching a show about the Okavango Delta in Africa. The delta has a climate that goes from warm to hot, and this area has extreme conditions from very dry to very wet seasons. In November and December, the rain comes in like a downpour, which provides much relief, especially for the animals in this area, as trillions of gallons of water rush over the land. While watching this program, I saw herds of what I believe were cattle-like animals running to and through this overflow of water. On land that was once extremely barren and dry, these animals were overtaken by the outpour of the life-giving power of water. Wow! These animals, including hippos, consciously run to and through this water. It was like God cracked the sky and simply poured out massive water onto the land as if He was pouring out a cold drink of water on an extremely hot day.

Have you ever felt like you are in an extremely dry place? While watching this show, I wondered what it was like to breathe the air in this area as the rain drew near. It likely felt like a deep breath of relief. Do you feel like you are in a situation now where you feel choked by the trials and challenges of life? Holy Spirit is speaking to you now. He has just used the climate of the Delta to show you what will happen if you hold on and continue to be patient.

Wait on God's timing of the rush of His water – His Holy Spirit, His blessing, His overflow. It's perfect. Get ready for it. Expect it. Look for it. Can you imagine what these animals felt as they sensed the shift and change in the air within the atmosphere? As they felt the distant rain in the wind and the raindrops splashing on them while they traveled and moved? (By the way, I saw the blue jay from Devotion #11 today.) The Spirit of the Lord is with you. Get ready to receive the outpour of His promises.

Scripture: John 7:38 *"He that believeth on me, as the scripture hath said, out of his belly shall flow rivers of living water."*

Prayer: Father, I thank you for the fragrance of rain I feel in the atmosphere. I even appreciate the dry and barren times in my life, because they allow me to appreciate when you bless me with your overflowing grace and mercy. You supply me with everything I need at the time you desire. Help me continue to show thankfulness during every trial, every point in my life that seems dry, and I will eagerly anticipate the rain of your Spirit. In Jesus' Name.

Run To The Water

DAY 13 DEVOTION

Your Walk Is as Unique as You Are

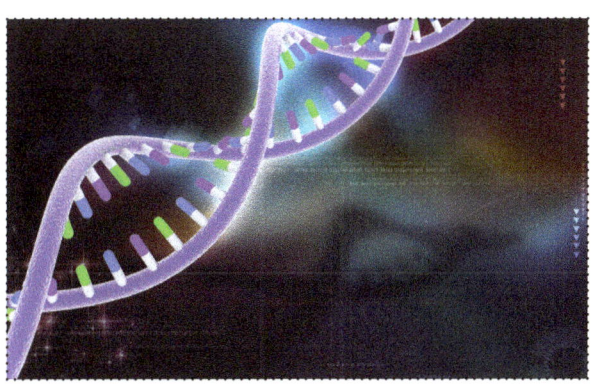

I walk my dog every morning (or at least I try to be as consistent as I can). She eagerly tugs at the leash, excited to go out to experience the morning air, or "the breath of God" as I like to call it. I often like to look up at the clouds when I take her for walks. I enjoy the tapestry of the beautiful art God dangles from His sky. One day, we took our normal route, and when we arrived at the end of the corner, I looked up toward the sky as I anticipated what I might see this time. Holy Spirit focused my attention on two clouds that seemed to stand out. These two clouds reminded me of DNA as they were shaped like a double helix. If we take a quick trip back to science class, we learned that DNA is the carrier of genetic information. It is part of what makes us who we are, both collectively and individually. It is present in nearly all living organisms, and it is part of how all of God's creation presents itself in a different way – from form to function. Look at the many different breeds of dogs, or the hundreds of different types of birds in the world, or all the different nationalities across the earth. It is the diversity of our God-created DNA.

And then Holy Spirit used the action of me walking my dog and the display of this double-helix formation in the clouds to speak to my heart. Holy Spirit said: *"Just as you walk your dog and notice what I show you in the clouds, I am showing you and reminding you that you are unique, fearfully and wonderfully made. And because I made you unique, your walk with me is destined to be unique. It will not be like anyone else's."*

> **Scripture: Jeremiah 29:11** *"For I know the thoughts I think toward you, saith the Lord, thoughts of peace, and not of evil, to give you an expected end."*
>
> **Prayer:** Father, thank you for the unique DNA you placed inside of me. If I start to compare myself to others or even compare my walk with others, may I be quickly reminded that it is your plan for all your creation to be unique and thus to have a unique path. May I always be in tune to the direction you want me to walk. In Jesus' Name.

Your Walk Is As Unique As You Are

DAY 14 DEVOTION

The Stomata of Laughter

While I was attending a dynamic worship conference, Holy Spirit allowed me to minister to a friend. I cherish those moments in corporate worship when the sound of heaven spreads through the atmosphere and

The Stomata Of Laughter

the rush of God's Holy Spirit fills the room. In those moments, the atmosphere is conducive for Holy Spirit to speak and for a mighty move of God to occur. During this moment at the conference, the glory of God was heavy in the room, and it seemed like everyone around me was overwhelmed with the Spirit.

As I stood next to my sister in Christ, even in that moment, Holy Spirit saw fit to download a comforting message to share with her. The beautiful thing was that the encouraging message Holy Spirit downloaded was in the form of an occurrence that happens in nature. I thought to myself, "Wow, how amazing that in this very moment, God, you are even using me to share a divine download." Holy Spirit spoke through me to my sister in Christ and said *"I am opening up the stomata of laughter in your life."* So of course, she kind of looked at me, not really understanding what stomata really are. I explained to her that stomata can be found on the back of a leaf. They cannot be seen with the naked eye. They are openings or pores that control the rate of gas exchange. These pores take in carbon dioxide and release oxygen, creating a synergistic relationship between humans and plants. We release the gas carbon dioxide, which most plants and trees need to grow and produce their own food – a process called photosynthesis.

Not to go too deep into the science lesson – the main thing Holy Spirit wanted to share was that He was going to open up the pores of laughter and joy back into her life. Once I explained a little about the function of the stomata and how it related to what Holy Spirit was saying to her, I could see her overcome with emotion. Tears started to roll down her face. She then understood the function of the stomata and how it related to what Holy Spirit downloaded and spoke. This would be the start of Holy Spirit continuing to use me to share downloads from nature to edify, exhort and comfort. I encourage you to start to learn more about different aspects of nature. I believe you will see, experience and hear Holy Spirit in a beautifully different way. In these moments Holy Spirit may even open up opportunities to minister to others.

> **Scripture: 1 Corinthians 14:3** *"But he that prophesieth speaketh unto men to edification, and exhortation, and comfort."*

> **Prayer:** Father, I thank you for the blessing of laughter and joy. I pray you continue to pour out your spirit of laughter and joy upon me. Help me to continue to learn more about the intricacies of nature and the form and function of how it all works to and for YOUR glory. I pray you will open up doors of opportunity for me to share with people the downloaded instructions and encouragement you artistically share through creation. In Jesus' Name.

The Stomata Of Laughter

DAY 15 DEVOTION

THE WIND OF HOLY SPIRIT

What do you think about when you think of the wind? Take a moment now... close your eyes... see the picture Holy Spirit just placed before you. You can even take a moment to draw what you see. Do you immediately see the vision of tree limbs blowing back and forth? Do you hear and imagine a blustering sound, or is there something else your mind sees when you think of "the wind"?

There is no right or wrong answer to these questions. The truth is, Holy Spirit can use any part of what *you* personally see, experience and feel to download divine instruction from heaven, through nature, to your heart. How heavenly rich is that!? Every personal message, including the context of what Holy Spirit shares, is so uniquely different. Allowing God through Holy Spirit to communicate His authentic message(s) is like a fingerprint. All fingerprints are different – there aren't any two that are the same!

> **Scripture: Psalm 78:26** *"He caused an east wind to blow in the heaven: and by his power he brought in the south wind."*
>
> **Prayer:** Father, I thank you for the heavenly richness all around me. Help me to open myself up to see and experience you in a different way. I pray for your power to fall as you, the Creator, open up even more revelation and Holy Spirit-downloaded wisdom. Allow God's fingerprinted messages and downloads to expand and go beyond any preconceived thoughts I may have. In Jesus' Name.

The Wind Of Holy Spirit

DAY 16 DEVOTION

Arrows of Praise

I enjoy fellowshipping with other ministries, and I often share the ministry of the art of dance as worship to God (Psalm 149:3). During a virtual worship service, the praise team at the church I was visiting was singing praises to God. They were on one accord, and you could tell their hearts were aligned and surrendered to God as their praises permeated not only the physical space we were in but the virtual space as well. In an atmosphere like this, Holy Spirit shows up in a mighty way, and He did. Even at the end of the service, the Spirit of God still lingered like the haze of mist after a downpour of cool rain on the hot cement of a steamy summer day. In the moments after the service ended, I was filled to overflowing, and God led me to share the Holy Spirit download with the entire praise team.

Holy Spirit said, *"Their praises were like arrows being fiercely propelled by the movement of the wind. Their songs of praise pierced the airwaves across social media. Even though the enemy may have been trying to shift the overall direction of these piercing songs of praise, and even if the wind was blowing fiercely in an opposing direction, the arrow of your praise, the breath, the words of God being sung supernaturally pierced the darkness. Holy Spirit reminded them to keep sending the songs and sounds of God into the atmosphere. I encouraged them to even hum and make a sound of praise in the atmosphere on a daily basis. I reminded the praise team that as breath and air is being inhaled into their earthly vessels and then released, they are actively releasing the power of God and destroying yokes of suicide, depression, anxiety, frustration and so much more."*

Arrows Of Praise

What I found interesting about what Holy Spirit shared with the praise team is that He encouraged them not only to continue to sing but also to hum and simply send out a sound. We *are* created by God. We *are* a part of God's creation. We *are* vessels of atmosphere changers. Sometimes we do not even know what to say or even pray, but Holy Spirit, our helper, does. You don't need to be on a formal praise team to muster up a heartfelt, Spirit-filled sound to God. Send it forth today! Allow the wind of the Spirit to pierce the darkness.

> **Scripture: Romans 8:26** *"Likewise the Spirit also helpeth our infirmities: for we know not what we should pray for as we ought: but the Spirit itself maketh intercession for us with groanings which cannot be uttered."*
>
> **Prayer:** Father, thank you for giving me the ability to open my mouth and sing to you, hum to you and just simply make a sound to you. I pray as I am led by the wind of your Spirit that my sounds of praise will be propelled forth into the atmosphere with a purpose to pierce the darkness and release the virtue of your presence in a mighty way. In Jesus' Name.

DAY 17 DEVOTION

Rest in Joy

I was in awe when I saw this. I mean, how could anyone miss this amazing view? Wherever I looked, I could see no end to where the joy rested. It's bright and radiant, lighting up the space it occupies. I immediately thought of the scripture about "joy coming in the morning" (Psalm

30)! Not like a trickle of joy, but more like a blanket of joy – a warm, fuzzy one. As I peer across this sea of joy, the vibrant color makes me feel alive. It reminds me of all the promises God has written in His Word.

Lots of things transpire in the morning. There is significance to the *morning* time. Think about it.... In the morning there is stillness in earth's atmosphere. In the morning there is water or dew on the grass. Father God takes time to moisten each blade of grass, one by one. By His Spirit, every blade of grass is *touched* by Him. But what happens during the time before the morning light or morning *joy*? In the evening, or several hours before daylight presses through the sky – I feel this is the time right before the manifestation of joy occurs. I believe Holy Spirit desires this waiting time to be a time of spiritual instruction.

> **Scripture: Psalm 30:5** *"For his anger endureth but a moment; in his favour is life: weeping may endure for a night, but joy cometh in the morning."*
>
> **Prayer:** Father, let me never take advantage of your joy that comes every morning. It is precious to me, and I will cherish it forever. I will look for joy in my morning, and when you bless me with it, I will pour it out on others who need it. May I show forth joy like never before. In Jesus' Name.

Rest In Joy

DAY 18 DEVOTION

THE SOUND OF FREEDOM

And then there was a sound! Often in the mornings, I play worship music to start and prepare for my day. On this particular day, I was listening to Maverick City's song entitled "Miracles." I went back into the bedroom where my husband was lying. I was led to sit beside him and take a moment to Selah and just listen and meditate on the melody of this song. It was filling the atmosphere of my house.

As I sat, I was led to open the window in my bedroom to allow some fresh air in. Still basking in the melody, spirit and message of this song, I heard a bird pierce the outside atmosphere with a sharp and distinct sound. I heard this as soon as I opened the window. It was as if this bird had started singing its own melody to the Father. There were other birds I heard outside chirping away, but *this* bird was offering and sending forth a different and more profound sound.

Holy Spirit then downloaded a question: *"What sounds are my people making to me to get my attention?"* Holy Spirit reminded me of a situation in the Bible, when Paul and Silas were in jail and they began to pray and sing praises to God. Well, what happened after they sent these sounds forth? The chains BROKE! A MIRACLE! Through their praises to the Father in that very moment, God delivered! [Acts 16:25-26] Imagine if we were to walk in a constant place of praise from the beginning of our day to the end, and as we go to work, school, etc., with the praises of God overflowing even from our countenance. Imagine the number of people you could help FREE!

What sound are you sending through the window of your heart? Is it inviting to others on the outside? Does it compel them to want to join in with you? Purpose to keep the sound of praise in your heart to help set people free.

Scripture: Acts 16:25-26 *"And at midnight Paul and Silas prayed, and sang praises unto God: and the prisoners heard them. And suddenly there was a great earthquake, so that the foundations of the prison were shaken: and immediately all the doors were opened, and every one's bands were loosed."*

Prayer: Father, I pray that you help me to stay in a place of praise to you. Even as I walk throughout this day, allow my countenance, my face, my mood, my emotions and my character to show forth your Praise, Glory and Goodness. As I offer you praise, I declare freedom for all people who come across my path today. In Jesus' Name.

The Sound Of Freedom

DAY 19 DEVOTION

Blooming in the Midst

I enjoy spending time with my family! We enjoy each other's company and the laughter we share together. One particular spring night, we were all sitting on the deck at home. It was a bit chilly, and we'd just had some cold rain showers come through. As I sat and looked out to the back yard, I noticed the rain clouds were still hovering over us. In this moment, Holy Spirit gave me a DOUBLE DOWNLOAD. This download was not only from what I would soon see in the sky – Holy Spirit's download and instruction were pulled from an experience I had earlier that day as well. I had no idea Holy Spirit would link two separate occurrences in one divine message. Allow me to begin by sharing the first Spirit-filled experience.

I always enjoy the presence of fresh flowers in my home, especially the really bright-colored ones. They bring life and energy to any space. While I was out quickly shopping for groceries before picking up my kids, I noticed these beautiful pink flowers for sale. They were bright pink tulips. Even the stem was a pretty, silky green color. After checking out, I gently placed the tulips on top of one of the grocery bags, and I started thinking of some locations in my home where I would display this beauty.

I did notice there were some bulbs that were not quite open when I placed them on top of the bag. After I picked up my kids from school, and a few open bags of chips later (they are always so hungry when I pick them up), we arrived home. As I started to take the bags out of the car, I immediately noticed that these same tulips that had half-open bulbs had already started to bloom. These same tulips I had placed on top of the grocery bag were not in a vase of water; however, their petals still pushed open and started to bloom, displaying the center of their sweetness with a fragrant aroma.

Now let's fast-forward to the evening family time I mentioned earlier. It will soon make sense as to why I shared this tulip experience first. As I noticed the rain clouds, I saw a double rainbow in the sky. It was one of the shortest rainbows I had ever seen. I immediately thought, "God's Covenant!" Then something interesting happened. As I continued to look at this rainbow, I noticed it was fading away and disappearing. I had never seen a rainbow appear and disappear that quickly. Then I looked to the left and saw a cloud shaped like the bulb of the flower I bought earlier that day. And just like that, Holy Spirit downloaded to my spirit: *"I have established my covenant with you, and my faithfulness will come through. Even when you may not immediately see my promises blooming before you, just know I am still here. I am working and still moving on your behalf. Even when you feel disconnected from the source, I will show you my glory, and you will still bloom in the midst."*

God can still bring life to situations where the source seems to be non-existent, dry or even void – just like the tulip flowers I laid across my grocery bag. They had no vase of water to be submerged in, but these flowers still had just enough of what they needed at that moment. Perhaps there was just enough water stored in the stem of these flowers to keep them from wilting and losing their leaves. Most of the time when I get flowers from the store, they look the exact same way when I bring them home. It's only when I place them in water that I start to see them open up and bloom. Not this time! God knew what He was planning to show and share with me later that evening. It was all Holy Spirit connected!

Scripture: 2 Corinthians 12:9 *"And he said unto me, My grace is sufficient for thee: for my strength is made perfect in weakness. Most gladly therefore will I rather glory in my infirmities, that the power of Christ may rest upon me."*

Prayer: Father, I thank you, for you are the source of everything I need. I will no longer look at what I do not physically have but will put my faith in the one and only provider. I bless you for the covenant of your promise you made with me. I pray now for the areas in my life that feel and seem hopeless. I decree and declare that you will supernaturally cause those places to bloom and blossom suddenly. They will flourish because you have made a covenant with me. I trust your will and know you never make any mistakes. Your favor is upon me. In Jesus' Name.

DAY 20 DEVOTION

HOLY SPIRIT GOES BEFORE ME

My husband, Steven, enjoys coaching and training kids in basketball. One spring afternoon, we found ourselves at the park for one of his training sessions. One of the reasons I came along was because I always enjoy watching him operate in his gift. This park had a walking trail, so I decided to get some steps in while he finished up the session. I walked across the side of the court cautiously to avoid getting hit with any air-bound basketballs (there were lots of people playing on the court that day). I have been on the receiving end of one of those air-bound basketballs – it smacked me right in my face, which left me with a very sore eye for the next few days and, needless to say, a broken pair of glasses – but that's a story for another day 😊. As I walked onto the trail, I thought to myself, "Should I go to the car and change into my other shoes?" I had on a pair of really comfortable sandals – the ones made with the very soft, cushiony part on the bottom of the shoe that almost conformed to my foot and that bounced back with each step. It was the very first time I had walked on this trail, so I didn't know what to expect. I know the details I am sharing might seem meaningless, but they *are* meaningful and significant because what Holy Spirit showed me and downloaded was so encouraging.

I probably took seven steps onto the trail, and there it was – a blue jay! It flew directly in front of me. It swooped down to my eye view and then swooped back up and perched on the top of a metal fence to my right. I looked up and thought about how this situation reminded me of what Holy Spirit spoke to me in the past (which I also shared in my Day 11 devotion).

This Holy Spirit download gave me a heap of encouragement: *"The Spirit that was with you when you looked out of your window from the comfort of your home* [read devotion Day 11 to get the full picture] *is the same Spirit that will go before you as you walk. I will prepare a place for you, prepare a place in the presence of your enemies. I go before you, stand before you and hover over you to watch and see what is coming to protect you, lead you and guide your footsteps to safety, even in the midst of what has happened in the past. Walk in comfort and knowing I am with you and Goodness and Mercy leads and follows you all the days of your life. Keep walking with me and serving me – the true and Living God. I am with you."*

Scripture: Psalm 23 *"The Lord is my shepherd; I shall not want. He maketh me to lie down in green pastures: he leadeth me beside the still waters. He restoreth my soul: he leadeth me in the paths of righteousness for his name's sake. Yea, though I walk through the valley of the shadow of death, I will fear no evil: for thou art with me; thy rod and thy staff they comfort me. Thou preparest a table before me in the presence of mine enemies: thou anointest my head with oil; my cup runneth over. Surely goodness and mercy shall follow me all the days of my life: and I will dwell in the house of the Lord for ever."*

Prayer: Father, I pray that whatever may be hindering me from moving forward and walking with you on a deeper and higher level will cease to have a hold on me. I bind fear in the name of Jesus, and I welcome and release the guiding presence of your anointing and protection over me now. Grace and Mercy follow me constantly. In Jesus' Name!

DAY 21 DEVOTION

SENT AND SET APART

Sometimes God will send you out on your own so you can have first choice. I will share more about what I mean by "first choice" in just a second. Oftentimes when we see birds eating in a field, they are in a flock, but this morning, I looked out my window and saw a little brown bird. The bird seemed so small amidst the large backyard it was walking through. It pecked around as if to be very selective about the food it was picking up. The bird took a couple more steps and then shifted in another direction, pecked some more in the grass, walked a bit more and reached toward the ground to eat a little more.

As I watched this bird choose its food, Holy Spirit spoke to me and said, *"Don't think just because I have sent you on your own that you are alone. I have sent you because I want you to have FIRST PICK."* Earlier this morning, I was thinking, dreaming and wondering about all God has planted in my heart to do here on earth (and honestly wondering how in the world I would accomplish it all). Have you ever had those thoughts? The truth is, you can accomplish all He has purposed in your heart to do. His Word says so in Ephesians 3:20: *"Now unto him that is able to do exceeding abundantly above all that we ask or think, according to the power that worketh in us."*

I continued to think and dream about how I could continue to use my gifts and talents for His Glory. Several thoughts ran across my mind: "Should I move forward with the visions I have? Is this truly what you want me to focus on in this season, Lord?" Holy Spirit reminds me of the scripture: *"Commit thy works unto the Lord, and thy thoughts shall be established"* (Proverbs 16:3). I think to myself, "It's new territory… what about all the other purposes and plans you have for me?"

Holy Spirit reminded me: "*I can do all things through Christ which strengtheneth me*" (Philippians 4:13). I think about how strength is physically manifested, and Holy Spirit gives an example of someone who is just starting to lift weights. They don't just wake up one day, able to lift a 50-pound weight with ease. The muscles have to get warmed up first, and then the power of repetition and consistently lifting the weights on a daily basis helps to build the physical muscle. And then what happens next? STRENGTH is manifested! What initially seemed to be a heavy load is now the manifestation of Christ's strength.

It is important to be selective with what you eat. Yes, literally, but I am also talking spiritually as well. God has placed us in this world, and He has given us a choice – just like the brown bird I saw walking in my back yard. Only you know where "this place" is. Don't just consume the first thing that is in front of you. Be selective. Be in tune to what God wants for you. Allow Him to lead you.

The truth is, you may have to walk away from something and even some people in order to go where He wants you to go – even if it means God sending you alone. Be careful, because people can distract you from what God wants you to focus on, even when their intentions seem to be harmless.

Scripture: 2 Timothy 3:16-17 *"All scripture is given by inspiration of God, and is profitable for doctrine, for reproof, for correction, for instruction in righteousness: That the man of God may be perfect, thoroughly furnished unto all good works."*

Prayer: Father, I pray you will show me where to go and the places not to go. Help me to put the truth of your Word into action. As I commit my works and all my thoughts to you, may I be ever so selective of what I choose to consume – whether it is what I watch on TV, what or whom I listen to and even who I chose to connect with. In Jesus' Name.

Sent And Set Apart

Receive YOUR Holy Spirit Downloads, NOW!

Your steps are divinely ordered by God, and He has told us that He walks with us on a daily basis. So think about it: God wants to be with us at all times, to lead and guide us. God didn't say "I will only be with you and lead you in the morning during your devotional time." He said, "I will never leave you or forsake you!" (Deuteronomy 31:6). How much PEACE is that! So, when you finish your morning devotional, God continually speaks and is with you at all times. He is a multisensory God. If you cannot see nature, perhaps you can hear nature – the birds, the wind, the ocean. Or if you cannot hear, perhaps you can touch – you can feel the morning dew on the grass and how each blade is saturated with the dew of His Presence, His Glory. Can you see now? Are you ready to hear from heaven through nature? Pay attention to the colors and textures of nature. God created it all to confirm and affirm that He will always be with us and is speaking to us constantly. Get ready for your own Holy Spirit Downloads!

www.ingramcontent.com/pod-product-compliance
Lightning Source LLC
Chambersburg PA
CBHW072010090426
42734CB00033B/2326